The Big Business Card

Promoting Your Business with a Book

By: Dale Anderson

Disclaimers

Income Disclaimer

This document contains business strategies, marketing methods and other business advice that, regardless of my own results and experience, may not produce the same results (or any results) for you. I make absolutely no guarantee, expressed or implied that by following the advice below you will make any money or improve current profits, as there are several factors and variables that come into play regarding any given business.

Primarily, results will depend on the nature of the product or business model, the conditions of the marketplace, the experience of the individual, and situations and elements that are beyond your control.

As with any business endeavor, you assume all risks related to investment of money based on your own discretion and at your own potential expense.

Liability Disclaimer

By reading this document, you assume all risks associated with using the advice given below, with a full understanding that you, solely, are responsible for anything that may occur as a result of putting this information into action in any way, and regardless of your interpretation of the advice.

You further agree that I cannot be held responsible in any way for the success or failure of your business as a result of the information presented below. It is your responsibility to conduct your own due diligence regarding the safe and successful operation of your business if you intend to apply any of our information in any way to your business operations.

Terms of Use

You are given a non-transferable, "personal use" license to this product. You cannot distribute it or share it with other individuals.

Also, there are no resale rights or private label rights granted when purchasing this document. In other words, it's for your own personal use only.

Table of Contents

Introduction

If you experience:

- Price resistance
- Fighting for sales with your competitors
- Problems differentiating yourself from the crowd

Read this book and find out exactly what you get and how you're going to be helped. I will go through all the processes step-by-step to show you what is done. Is this the only way to write a book? No! Is this the only way to publish a book? No! Is this the only way to promote a book? No! It's my way, it's effective and your book gets done. If you follow my suggestions, it will increase your business; bring in more leads, more prospects and more sales of your products and services.

You will learn what to do by reading this book, I will show exactly what you have to do in order to get your book written, published and promoted. I will document step-by-step exactly what I do when I write a book, when I published a book, and the things that I do promote my book so you can do the same thing.

There are many elements to publishing a professional-looking book. However, you do not need to be an expert in book publishing to release a high-quality book. You can have me take care of many of the details of content, formatting, editing, cover creation and marketing, while you reap the many benefits of having a published book.

You will soon learn that having a published book gives you instant creditability when it comes to being the expert in your niche. Let's look at this from a customer's point of view. If you need to sell your home and you were looking for the best real estate agent and Agent A hands you a business card and Agent B hands you a published book, who would you be more inclined to hire? Even if you hate reading, I bet you answered Agent B.

This works the same for any niche in any industry.

The great part about writing a book is that it is even easier than you think once you really understand how to do it. There are methods and techniques to writing a book very quickly (even quicker than seven days!).

You will want a published book to physically hand people for whatever message you are trying to convey. It is quite an accomplishment to have a published book and most people will go through their entire lives not knowing what it feels like to be a published author.

This should be very exciting for you because the fact is that most people are not walking around with a published book so you can quite possibly be the only professional in your town that has one.

Why Publish A Book

So, why publish a book? Publishing a book is a great way to grow your business. Handing people a copy of your book, or pointing them to your book listing on Amazon will reinforce the fact that you are an expert in your field.

Publishing a book, and having copies available for potential clients will not only demonstrate your expertise and authority, but it is also a great way to educate potential buyers, answer common questions about your services, and get prospects to commit to the next level of doing business with you.

Nearly any profession or business can benefit from having a published book available to the general public. Whether you are a service provider such as a real estate agent or a dentist, a small business owner, or a salesperson, you can leverage the authority of having your own book to educate, impress, and persuade potential, new, and current clients.

Writing a book will benefit you and your business by increasing your expert status. When that happens, you can reap these benefits:

Charge More Money

If you needed a plumber to install your new jet-tub, which of the following plumbers would you hire? The one who wrote the book about jet-tub installation, or one who did not? Which plumber do you think would charge more? Authors are considered experts on their subject and experts get to charge more for their services.

Increase Your Number of Clients

Even if you just give your book away, you will become *the person* who knows about your industry, and every time someone puts your book on the shelf, they are advertising you and your business!

Be Invited to Speaking Events

Even when no one has read your book, if you are an author, people want to hear from you. When you speak, you are seen as an authority on your topic and you will attract more customers.

Reputation Management

Being proactive is the best way to manage your business's reputation. Your authorship page, and sometimes your book's sales page, will show up on the first page of Google. That is definitely better than your latest divorce proceedings.

What Kind Of Book To Write

Write A Skinny Book

A book based on your customer. We're making a skinny book so we do not bore the reader and we also want you to finish the book, this is not to be a big novel, this is a book written strictly for your customer, client, or patient so that you can help provide solutions to problems that they have.

It is that simple, you're not trying to sell a lot of copies of these books, you're not trying to become famous as an author, you're simply using this book as a means to provide value to your leads, prospects or existing customers. By helping them, you will automatically promote your business, your products and services.

Your book In Print

As we move towards digitizing everything, it sometimes becomes difficult to think about the benefits of older technologies or methods. In this instance, we are talking about a print book. Yes, eBooks or digital books are easier to distribute and they take up zero physical space, but there are some elements that an eBook just cannot replicate, just try handing out eBooks. It can't be done, unless the prospect has the reader or computer to view the eBook. This is especially true if you are a local expert in any niche. If you want to expand your personal brand, then print books are the way to go.

Tangible and Physical

A book is something real that you can touch and see. Unlike an eBook that only exists as a file, a print book is something that has weight. Giving someone a real book increases the likelihood that they will read it. Also, unlike eBooks that are easy to lose beneath files and folders, a book takes up space. Clients can always pick it up and read it at their leisure. In their office, home, shop, even their bathroom library.

More Benefits Of A Print Book

Credibility

One of the major perceived differences between print books and eBooks is that eBooks can be made by anyone. From the best to the worst writers, anyone can publish an eBook. While print-on-demand technology allows you to print a book without going through publishers and editors, most people do not realize this.

Publishing a print book shows that you are serious about your expertise. It shows that you have gone through the publishing hoops to get your information out there. Experts need as much credibility as possible and print books produce that perfectly. Plus, people tend to expect better information and more details from printed materials; this allows you to show off your knowledge and experience.

This book will position you ahead of your competition if you have a book and they do not, you automatically are top dog because by writing this book you have established yourself with credibility that published authors are usually given, and looked on with respect as experts in your field.

If you provide solutions to people's problems they will get to know like and trust you and eventually do business with you. The only requirement on your part is that you have something that you provide to your customers that really helps and if you don't have anything like that, a book is not going to help you because you have nothing to write about but if you can honestly say; I provide good service, wonderful product, customer service, even any unique features, you can develop a book from that.

Mix Digital and Physical

This is one benefit that has nothing to do with perception or belief. You can mix digital marketing right into your print book. Just add the address of a website, social media page, or blog to bring people to your online space, usually looks like www.ipublishbooks.com

Branding

Branding is all about solidifying your presence and showing people that you are trustworthy when it comes to your niche. Print books have more power behind them, and it gives people something to walk away with. They will start to trust your brand more and more as they look at the book. It's like you are going with them, your message is being reinforced as they read your book.

Engagement

People are more engaged by print books. They give them more time and they carefully read each word. It has been shown that people really read print books, but skim eBooks and digital pages. This gives you the opportunity to get your potential clients engrossed in you and your business.

Print books have the advantage of being physical and are able to truly engage readers so that they fall in love with your personal brand. While these books are a little harder to make and distribute, print-on-demand service providers make the job much easier and more affordable.

There are a number of companies that will allow you to self-publish your book, by that I mean they will take your book print it for you and allow you to be your own publisher. Now the company that I have chosen to use is Createspace they are a division of Amazon and you can sell your book on Amazon once it's printed by Createspace so this will also put your book on the shelves of the world's largest retailer as a bonus. You probably won't sell many books from that listing, but just pointing it out to prospects will impress the hell out of them.

You simply go to createspace.com and create your own account and they provide step-by-step instructions that allow you to eventually upload your book and get it published. The great thing about Createspace is you can order one copy, or you can order 100 copies, rather inexpensively and have them shipped to your address and at the same time sell your book for almost any price directly on Amazon.

For example if I write a skinny book with less than 50 pages I can probably order 100 books shipped to my home or my place of business for around $2.50 each. Getting my book shipped to me at those prices allows me to distribute my book for free if I wish, so I can promote my own products and services.

Who Will Be Interested In What I Write?

The people who you wrote your book for will be interested, your book will provide help on a topic that they're interested in, you are solving those people's problems and anyone who has a problem is interested in finding a good solution. If you have an existing business you already helping people, so your book just simply informs them of all the ways you can help them and it will also attract people who are unaware of what you are doing, to come to your place of business and become one of your clients or customers.

By concentrating on problem solving your book will automatically attract the right people to your business. The goal is to let people know what you can help them with; of course you can only help them if you are actually solving problems. One interesting side effect of writing your book will be, you'll come to understand the needs of your customers better, you will think of more ways that you can help them, I believe you may even modify the way you do business so you can provide more and better services for your customers.

What Are The Benefits Of Educating Prospects Or Customers?

Your book will answer most of your prospects questions prior to their purchasing your product or service.

It will reduce sales questions during your sales process, presentations and also act as an instruction or operations manual

You can also set up expectations between you and your customers. What you expect them to provide, what they can expect you to provide and go into great detail on both.

If you wish you could even go into an explanation of your offers for example, you've explained what they get in your bronze plan, you can also tell them what they can get in your silver plan, which includes your bronze plan plus ABC.

Let your imagination roam, you could make an offer for purchasing your bronze plan today and getting your silver plan as a bonus for absolutely zero additional cost if they are prepared to buy before leaving the store, office, room, or seminar.

I think a good thing to include in your book is, your hours of operation, tell them why you work those hours. Let them understand what they can expect. If you close your business at 5:30 every night tell them you do this so your employees can be home with their family for dinner.

If you stay open till 10 o'clock every night tell them you do this so you can serve them better. People will adjust their expectations if you simply explain why, they may not agree, they may want you to have longer hours, they may want you to open up earlier, however a simple explanation of why can eliminate any misunderstandings or conflicts.

Explain any special services that you offer, if you offer 24 hour emergency service tell them that, and what the response time is. These are things are very important to prospects and you have a great opportunity to beat your own drum in this book.

Putting Your Book's Content Together

There are a number of ways you can create compelling and interesting book content that will let people know more about you, your profession, and the services that you have to offer. In this section, I will share some ways you can get your content into your book.

Writing it Yourself

The first and the most straightforward way is to just write it yourself. However, before you do this, you will want to save yourself hours of heartache and frustration by starting with an outline of what you want to cover. Once you have put together an outline, you can sit down at the computer and start filling in parts. Feel free to jump around—It is easier start with the sections that most interest you. You do not need to start from the beginning and work your way to the end.

You can use nearly any type of word processing program or text editor to write your book. However, one of the best platforms is Microsoft Word, as this program makes it relatively easy to format your book for publishing.

Dictation and Transcription

If sitting down at the computer is something that seems overwhelming, or something you are not comfortable with, a great way to get your content into your book quickly is to 'talk' your content. You can do this in a number of different ways.

You can use a computer dictation program and talk into the microphone. This type of program will transcribe your words automatically into your document. The most well-known program is Dragon Naturally Speaking. The newer versions have a high accuracy rate, and make it easy to create your book.

You can also use a more low-tech method, and just speak your thoughts directly into a tape recorder. If you do this, you will want to make sure you organize and label each section. For example, you will want to have a detailed outline and make sure you identify which part of the outline you are dictating before you start each section. While this can be very convenient, because you do not need to be in front of the computer, you will need to spend the extra time and expense of getting your content transcribed. There are a number of transcription companies available who can transcribe your content into a document.

Working With Me

The easiest and best solution is to have me help write or produce your content for you. Plus, you need to make sure you have all the additional parts of your book such as the front and the back cover. In addition, you will need to make sure that your book is professionally formatted, edited, and published. There are a lot of steps here, and it is best to work with someone like myself who can handle all of this for you.

The Interview Method

One easy way to create high-quality content with me is the interview method.

The best way to get the majority of your book content is to be interviewed and then have the content transcribed into a book. I can schedule a few sit-down sessions with you, where I ask questions and record your responses.

You can do this in person with a tape recorder or a microphone, or even right from your phone or computer.

I will then take the audio from the interview and have it transcribed, edited, proofread, and formatted for publishing

What Content Should You Include in Your Book?

FAQs and SAQs

The easiest way to start writing this book is simply write about your customers questions often we call these FAQs frequently asked questions, answer at least ten of them.

Then answer at least 10 SAQs should ask questions as often your customers do not understand what is really important and you can provide them this valuable information in your book

More FAQs can be found by visiting sites where people ask questions and include additional FAQs for the subject of the book.

Some places to find FAQs include answer websites like Yahoo Answers, industry-specific forums, and social media platforms.

For example, LinkedIn has a variety of industry-specific groups where people post content and provide information. In addition, they also have many experts asking and answering questions in their field.

Sample FAQs & SAQs

What do you mean a customer focused book?

19

The customer will write most of the content because we will only add content the customer has provided for us with their questions and requests.

What are you selling?

My services to help you publish a book that will show your prospects and even current customers that you are an authority in your field and can provide solutions for their problems

Why do you call the book "The Big Business Card"?

Because most of us have tried to put our important information on a business card and have filled up the front of the card and then run out of space on the back too and still had to leave some important information off the card, why not include everything with a book! You never have to agonize about what to eliminate.

I want to tell my story in the book too, can I do that?

Sure you can tell your story, but at the back of the book after you have answered most of your prospects questions and have shown them solutions for their problems. Then they will actually want to know more about you. Remember to share your experience and stories throughout the book if they illustrate solutions for the prospect reading your book.

I just sell gift baskets

I don't provide solutions for anyone, so how can a book help my business? Well first of all I would suggest that you do provide a solution for someone looking for a gift in the form of a "gift basket". In the book you could answer the following questions what do you have for:

- Valentine's day

- My mom

- A meat eater

- A vegetarian

- A diabetic

- A child

- My wife

- A graduate

- Going back to school

- My boss

- A going away present

- A coming home gift

The more good ideas you put in your book, the more sales you will make and possibly create a customer that will return again and again. Now I do not know much about the gift basket business but you do and could create some great specialty baskets and then tell about them in your book.

I just clean houses what could I possibly write about?

Answer questions like:

• Will you clean offices?

• Will you clean my shop?

• What type of cleaners do you use?

• Are the cleaning supplies eco-friendly

• What hours are you available?

• How often will you clean my house?

• Will you clean neglected and filthy rental units?

• Is it just you or do you have people that you hire that will be in my home?

• Do you do second story windows?

• Will you clean out my garage?

• Can you get the stains out of my carpet?

• Can you power wash my driveway and patio area?

- Do you do dishes, laundry, shopping?

- How do you screen your employees?

- Will my valuables in my home be safe?

My mother cleaned, other people's homes for years and sometimes cooked for them or their kids, so I know the list of provided services can be long, so put it in your book.

What will a book do for an attorney?

Not much if you are just an attorney, but if you specialize in some form of law practice, we have something to work with. Even if you are just beginning to develop a specialty you can explain your services in your book. A divorce attorney will ask and answer a whole different set of questions than say a criminal defense attorney. You can remove the mystery shroud for your practice and save time too by simply telling potential clients how it all works. The initial consultation cost this much, per visit, per hour, research and investigation of your case will cost this much.

I had an opportunity to talk to an attorney who accidently developed a specialty of a land use and zoning practice in our county. He researched one case and learned the rules for the county and the hoops that needed jumping through and that led to more cases till he was "making a very good living".

Now he did all that by word of mouth, a book could have taken him to the next level simply answering questions like:

• Can zoning laws be challenged?

• Can I change the land use classification of my property?

• The city annexed my farm and does not allow farm animals, can they do that?

• My property has been zoned as a watershed area and now the county wants me to upgrade my septic system and I cannot afford the $20,000 cost, what can I do?

• I own 40 acres and want to develop home sites on it, I am having a problem finding out how to get started. What do you suggest?

These questions can be written in a straight Q&A format or in story form, your choice either works.

If you have handled a similar case before, the last question could take the story form as follows:

In one case I had an older man who was a retired farmer and wanted to sell part of his farm for residential home sites. He had his land in open space so he had to pay 5 years of back taxes based on the difference between farm and developable property.

We then were able develop a plan for 7 home sites that was eventually approved by the building and codes department. I should be noted that this process took over a year to complete and had an upfront cost to survey, get a verifiable water supply, get approved septic systems, and build an approved road to all home site parcels.

Because we followed all zoning laws and building codes this retired farmer was able to sell the land parcels at a nice profit in a short period time.

Or the Q & A format similar to this:

I own a 40 acre farm and want to develop home sites on it. I am having a problem finding out how to get started. What do you suggest?

• If your farm is in open space you will need to take it out. You will have to pay 5 years of back taxes based on the differential.

• Get your development plot approved

• Verify potable water availability, either well or certified water system hookup for each home site

• A county approved septic system plan

• Build an approved road to each home site

• The above may take over a year to complete and all must be completed and paid for before any home sites can be sold.

• The upfront costs can be substantial but so can the profits, but it does take both time and money.

Pick questions that come up often so you can hand prospects a book upfront then answer more detailed questions later when they qualify as a serious prospect by:

• Attending a seminar

• Joining a conference call

• Signing up for your workshop

• Subscribing to your newsletter or email list

• Buying a product or service

• Joining a coaching program

• Scheduling an appointment

Many of you may already have a FAQ sheet or webpage so your job prior to your interview or writing your book is greatly simplified.

How To Expand Your Answers

If you choose to work with me I will draw out more details for each FAQ by asking questions.

For a home remodeler a good question might be: I want to remodel my kitchen can you do the whole job for me?

Yes

(me) You do everything?

Well not everything, I subcontract out the electrical and flooring.

(me) The electrical must be done by a state certified electrician which I am not.

(me) So why can't you do the flooring?

I can but my knees hurt, and I have a flooring guy that does beautiful work.

(me) do you build the cabinets yourself?

No it is not cost effective for me to build cabinets onsite when there are so many cabinet shops that can build custom cabinets at reasonable prices and if money is an issue big retail outlets supply good quality at cheap prices.

(me) do you work time plus materials or do you bid the whole completed kitchen labor and materials included?

Either way works for me however it is usually simpler and cheaper to go time plus materials as I don't need to pad the bid price to handle unforeseen problems like a rotten floor or non-compliant electrical problems.

Now I will change the original answer from a simple yes to something like this:

I certainly can do a complete kitchen remodel for you. I use a state certified electrician to do all the electrical so your kitchen wiring is safe and code compliant. I have a flooring guy that is the best I have ever seen do your floors for you. I will go with you to select your cabinets; you choose the quality and price to order and I will take care of installing them. I prefer to work on a time plus material basis, but can also give you a bid on the completed kitchen. You will have to select the quality, brand and sometimes model number of the following items:

- Refrigerator
- Sink
- Light fixtures
- Garbage disposal
- Trash compactor
- Counter tops
- Cabinets
- Cabinet hardware knobs and drawer pulls
- Microwave
- Stove

I suggest you select and pay for as many of the items as you can, no need for you to pay me to shop, or incur the expense of my running your purchases through my books, keeps me working in the kitchen.

Other Good Thing To Include

Tear-off pages these are pages that you can include in your book there are meant to be cut out or torn out of the book by your prospect or customer.

Coupons for your products or services make your book more valuable, if discounts are substantial and valuable, think out of the box here as you may very well justify discounted or even free exams, evaluations, analysis, or reports, to acquire new customers or clients.

Map to your location got to get them in the door so tell them where to go and how to get there.

Business cards create a page that looks like a business card so they can clip it out to use

Flow charts and diagrams remember a good picture can be worth a thousand words

Tickets for tradeshows or seminars if they like your book they may very well make special effort to come see you at these events.

List of your products and services let them know everything you have available for them.

Schedule of upcoming events, let them see where you will be and how engaged and busy you are, remember you can easily update your book when you add events.

Basic tips for that topic everyone needs to know (and in many cases, probably does know. Your basic tip will reassure the latter category of reader that you know what you are talking about)

Lesser-known tips that are potentially highly valuable—The sort of tips that can make the reader say, "Wow. It was worth buying the book just for that tip!"

"Insider" tips that the reader would never have found through regular channels. For this, you either need to have mastery of the topic yourself and be sharing years of experience, or interview someone who is either a master or has simply done the thing your reader is struggling to learn.

Additional Book Elements

Now that you have your book's content written, you also want to include important additional elements that make a book into a book. I can take your recorded or written content and assemble these other elements together to make a complete book.

Your Title

Your Title should be strong, short, simple, catchy (E.g. "Juice Fasting 101"), memorable, striking, and easy-to-remember. Make sure it contains keyword(s) if possible.

Your Sub-Title

A Sub-Title provides a way to expand on a really eye-catching Title without weakening it.

After the Title has grabbed their attention, your Sub-Title allows you to tip the reader off to what your book is really about. You don't always need one... but it's a good option to consider.

Your Introduction

Tell the reader:about:

- A few (or less) personal details about you that they can identify and connect with
- What motivated you to write this book for them

- What you intend to share
- What you hope they will get out of the book

Your Legal Disclaimer

You need to include legal disclaimers. They need to assert copyright ("all rights reserved").

Your Table of Contents (TOC)

Proper formatting is crucial as you want your book to look professional. Let me handle your book formatting for you.

When your book content concludes, there are three more optional sections you may wish to add...

Recommended Resources:

Here is where you can put links to your other products or website... Or to those of people you are partnering with.

Remember that all these elements should:

- Tie in together and read as a cohesive "whole"
- Be necessary to the flow and coherence of your book
- Enhance – not distract from – your "story"
- Help protect you and your book legally

However, you do not need to include every one. Include allowed calls to action within your book, Include allowed links within your book (especially at the end, or under "Resources" if appropriate).

Remember, your book structure is part of your book's personality, these elements can all be easily handled with me. Once I have your content, I can insert and prepare all of these elements that go into creating a book.

Including A Call To Action In Your Book

One of the main purposes of your book is to generate more customers and sales. You should include a strong call to action inside your book so readers can take the next step. This is a major part of your book that you do not want to leave out.

You can do several things such as:

- Ask readers to leave a review and share your book on social media
- Include a coupon or an incentive for them to try out one of your services
- Offer them something for free that they can redeem, such as a free consultation
- Provide a link for them to subscribe to your newsletter or mailing list, make sure to offer a free gift for them in return.

What If I Make A Mistake?

Your book will never be perfect, you will never say everything just the right way, you will never include everything you should have and you might even make a spelling error.

So what, the important thing is to get your book out there in the real world in front of those eyeballs that you want to contact and the nice thing is with Createspace you can fix anything you want to fix, once you discover your spelling errors, your grammar errors, your delivery errors you just make the change prior to printing your next book.

For The spelling and grammar Nazis out there you can spend six months getting everything as close to perfect as you can and I'll guarantee you it won't be perfect or you can put out your best effort and get your book out there in front of those eyeballs and promote your business. Otherwise you will miss out on all the profits that you could've made from promoting your business with your book for six months, even a year. Some people take five years to write a book you shouldn't take more than 30 days, and have your book written, published, printed and be out promoting your business in your community.

I can have your book professionally edited. Most people are familiar with copy editors, but that is just one type of editor that can help perfect your manuscript. This is a short list of the different types, so that you know who to look for. This is another task you can hand off to me. I will identify the types of editing you need and make sure your book is professionally edited.

Copy Editor

This is the most common type of editor, and it is the one that most people think of. They tend to be in the middle of the editing process. Most of them will fix grammatical and spelling mistakes, but there are some that leave that to proofreaders. All of them will comment on the writing itself. For example, they will say that a certain sentence does not make much sense given the style of the piece. They will also look for problems with details and ensure consistency from beginning to end.

Proofreader

Many people confuse proofreaders with editors due to their similar roles. Both of them look for grammatical errors. While this is a secondary job for copy editors (the primary one is ensuring consistency and perfecting the story and writing itself), it is the primary task for a proofreader. They are only concerned with spelling, commas, spaces, and other similar problems. They are often the last step of the editing process because they ensure that nothing has been missed by other editors.

Publishing Your Book

Publishing Considerations

Once your book files are created and edited, it is time to go ahead and get your book finalized for publication. I can take these additional steps so your book is all ready to go on the market.

Obtaining an ISBN for Your Book

You will need to obtain a ISBN number for your book. You have two options when it comes to this. You can shell out the cash to buy your own or you can opt to be assigned a free ISBN through the publishing distribution channel you are using to make your book available for sale.

Createspace offers free ISBNs for self-published books. There is no disadvantage to choosing a free ISBN, rather than buying one except Createspace will be listed as publisher instead of you.

Pricing your eBook

Obviously you have sorted out most of the little details for your book prior to this step in the self-publishing process.

You have chosen a descriptive, suitable title that you believe best conveys the story told in your book. You have obtained a professional-looking cover design to represent it visually to potential customers and readers. The interior of your book is properly formatted, however there is only one small, but very important, detail left to decide. That, of course, is how much you are going to charge for your book. This requires a bit of thought, and demands that you take a few different factors into consideration. I can also give you some suggestions.

The best thing about this decision is that you are able to change it at any time, and by any amount you wish. I like to set a reasonable price high enough that I can offer a good discounted price for seminar or meeting attendees. I have this book price set right now for $15 so I can offer a discount price of $5 if I wish.

Ordering Copies of Your Book

You can also easily order copies of your physical book. According to Createspace: "Orders you place for your title are referred to as "Member Orders." When you order copies of your own book, you pay just the fixed and per-page charges plus shipping and handling. Use our calculators to see your per-book, proof order cost, and shipping and handling costs." My first set of books cost less than 3$ each and that did include shipping. If you don't think you can pay $3 for new customer acquisition, or customer retention, perhaps a new line of business should be considered. Remember we are not trying to make money from book sales but from backend sales to our customers.

What Do I Do With My Book After It Is Published?

You have a choice of giving it away or selling your book, your call. I usually do a bit of both. I can retail my book for say $15 and yet still order and ship to myself for much less, depending on quantity and number of pages, usually $3 to $4.

Remember our plan is to make money on our backend product or service, not on book sales although that too can happen, just don't plan on it.

Do come up with a plan to get eyeballs on it, circulate your book every place you can. I suggest you start with local offline methods first and then add any internet marketing methods that appeal to you

If I don't sell my book for cash, I get something in trade, I always get their name, and email address along with permission to email them. Other things I may ask for are:

- Appointment to give my presentation
- Phone number to call them
- Sign them up for my newsletter
- Sign them up for my seminar or tele-seminar

I sell my book:

- At seminars
- At speaking engagements
- At teleseminars
- On my book website
- In my newsletter
- In my auto responder messages
- In my e-course

You might consider:

- Flea markets
- Your office, store or reception area
- Booth at trade shows or conventions

The possibilities are limited only by your imagination so dream a little bit think of ways that you can sell or give away your book to promote your business.

Do I Have To Promote My Book?

Yes unfortunately, even though your book will be listed on amazon, there are tens of thousands of nonfiction books competing with your book for those eyeballs

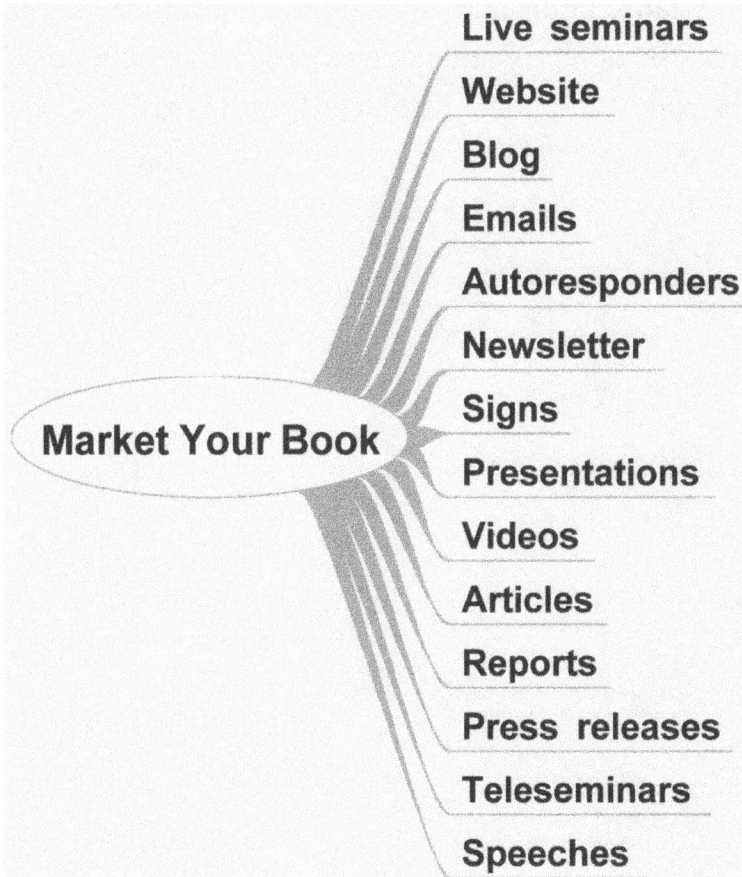

Market Your Book
- Live seminars
- Website
- Blog
- Emails
- Autoresponders
- Newsletter
- Signs
- Presentations
- Videos
- Articles
- Reports
- Press releases
- Teleseminars
- Speeches

Think local in your own community, concentrate on marketing methods that you can use but others outside your area can't or find difficult to do.

Ads in local newspapers, penny saver classifieds, magnetic door signs, local online directories, road signs, speaking to local groups; the list goes on and on.

Narrow your niche if your book is about hair products advertise for spas, beauty salons, beauty shops, beautician schools and wig shops. Concentrate on your own niche don't try and get everybody to read your book you want people who need your expertise.

Selling and Marketing Your Book

In Author Central

If you have written a book and placed it in Amazon's regular book storefront, you need to create an Amazon Author's Page at Author Central.

If you do not create one, people may still click on your name, hoping to see more information. A popup will appear, inviting the reader to visit your Amazon Page.

If you have created an Author's Page, your reader will click on your name when browsing a catalogue offering and a slightly different popup will show your Author Page profile photo.

Your Author Page photo and bio is a chance to:

- Connect personally to your readers
- Provide social validation
- Stamp yourself more securely into your reader's memory by putting a face to a name

You will also be able to create a blog and set up its RSS feed at your Author's Page as well as your own custom Author Page URL. I can create the necessary elements needed for an Amazon Author Central page and can also optimize it for the best results.

Do not neglect this fabulous promotional tool and resource. Your properly-optimized Amazon Author Page will help bond your readers to you, help convince readers to choose you over your competition, and will definitely help promote your books for years to come.

Setting Up a Website

You want to include any book testimonials and reviews from your own sales page on your site. Plus, you can use your Amazon link to promote your own book. You can use an Amazon widget that features your book and you could recommend closely related books as well.

Consider including the following details on your website:

- Contact Info
- Detailed description of your book: the more details the better; make it enticing
- Feature your name prominently
- Show your social media accounts so people can join you
- Offer a free chapter via an email opt-in to build your fan list
- Add a blog section only if you intend to publish to it regularly

Social Media Marketing

One of the best ways to start promoting your book is by using social media sites. You want to make use of Facebook, Google+, Twitter, and LinkedIn, and you may want to consider using Pinterest if you have images and photos that you can share.

Remember that on social sites you want to do a ton of sharing. So it is a great idea to share a little about how you became an author, what inspired you to write this book, and more. The main problem with social sites is that they can eat up your time. Work with me to setup your social media presence, I can also create and post regular content to your social media accounts.

Press Releases and Announcements

Doing a press release is a good way to promote your book. It is possible that a large magazine or TV station may see your release and contact you for an interview.

Google Hangouts, YouTube, and Webinars

Many authors have made use of marketing venues such as using Google+ Hangouts and Webinars. This method may or may not suit you, depending on your personality, but they are an excellent method of getting exposure, again I can help you do some of these.

Book Trailers

Book trailer videos are another great promotional item that you can use. You can make these short videos yourself or get someone to do them for you. Once uploaded to YouTube, you can embed the trailer on your Amazon author site and your own website and social pages. There is absolutely no reason why you cannot produce more than one book trailer video, either.

Guest Posts and Blog Tours

Another way to get attention for your new book is by offering to write guest posts on other websites and blogs. This works extremely well for numerous authors, and guest-posting allows you to help offer your expertise to a certain group of people.

The majority of blog owners will allow you to have one link in the bio area of your guest post, where you can link back to your author blog. This will help boost your site in the search engines and gain your additional visitors to your site.

Example Tear Out Pages

These pages are meant to be torn or cut out of your book to be used as a handy reference, admission to events, discount coupons, let your imagination run free on these ideas

Tear off Phone # Tab

Call me if you would like a copy of my book |
The Big Business Card

830-243-2598

830-243-2598

830-243-2598

830-243-2598

830-243-2598

830-243-2598

830-243-2598

830-243-2598

830-243-2598

830-243-2598

830-243-2598

830-243-2598

830-243-2598

Map To My Horse Farm

420 Windy Hill

Seguin Texas 78155

Address & Business Hours:

420 Windy Hill
Seguin Texas 78155

Tuesday thru Thursday

9AM to Noon

Tear Out This Coupon

Good for:

$100 Discount

on Silver Package

Please note that this coupon must be presented prior to your first book copy interview

Tear Out This Coupon

Good for:

$250 Discount

on Gold Package

Please note that this coupon must be presented prior to your first book copy interview

Free Admission

To Dale Anderson's

Promote Your Business With A Book

Monthly Seminar

Dale will explain **The Big Business Card** marketing system and how it can improve customer retention and new customer acquisition while increasing profits too.

Call for time and location

830-243-2598

Free 30 Minute Phone Consultation

With Dale Anderson

Find out if **The Big Business Card** marketing system is right for your business. Dale will answer your questions and explain the concept behind the system and how it may help you. You are under no obligation to buy anything, however if you feel your business can be helped by promoting it with a book, Dale will take additional time to explain your options.

Call to schedule your consultation

830-243-2598

Quick Application for Interview

Fill out and mail to Dale Anderson
420 Windy Hill, Seguin Texas 78155

Your Name:|

_____

Business Name:

_____

Phone#:_____

Email address:_____

Website:_____

Comments:

First Month of Online Group Coaching Free!

use code **777** in subject line of email and send to:

thebigbusinesscard@gmail.com

You will receive an email for time and location of each weekly coaching session. The venue will change from time to time a skype call, a teleconference call, the times and day will usually remain the same if possible.

Things I Offer

(limited availability)

Autoresponder Management: Setup an email series for your book and write broadcast emails that suck in new customers and clients for your business

Create a Blog for your profession or industry

Website Setup and Management: Create the basic standard website pages and add content monthly or weekly

Write Articles and Reports: based on your business niche and distribute them through your blog, autoresponder and local directories

Video Creation for your business and upload to your youtube account and your website.

Private Coaching: for those wanting to take their business to the next level through proven online and offline marketing methods that work.

Resources I Use

Aweber autoresponders

Hostgator webhosting

Weebly webhosting

PayPal payment processing

Createspace publishing

oDesk transcription and editing

Gmail webmail

Google Search web research

Amazon web storage, tools and supplies

Conclusion

Self-publishing a book is a powerful way to show off your expertise, establish your authority and grow your business. Being able to leverage expert author status will open up many more doors and opportunities for you than you may have ever imagined. With this guide, and my services, you have all the tools and resources necessary to make your book a reality. Remember your book is the perfect foot in the door tool and is so easy to use.

I have decided to include a report I wrote sometime back because it does a good job of summarizing what your own book can do for you.

Seven Good Reasons To Promote Your Business With A Book

Reason #1 your own book gives you *credibility*. Writing, publishing, and promoting a book of your own will increase your credibility because; people believe written words more than they believe what you say. Because you wrote a book they believe you must know what you're talking about, this assumption is made by most of us when we know somebody is a published author. Being a published author now elevates you above your competition, if your competition does not have a book, you have just got yourself a leg up on them, congratulations.

Let's say you have a your book laying on the counter of your business, you have it for sale, or you are giving it away to people who show interest, the mere fact that people see your book lying there with an interesting title, your name as the author and maybe your picture on the front or back cover, has just established you as an expert in your industry before they even talk with you.

Reason #2 is *reciprocity*, when you give your book to somebody, there is something about the human mind, personality, or spirit that demands that they give something back. If you give them your book that solves problems for them, they feel an obligation to give something back in return, in other words they reciprocate, perhaps they give you an appointment, listen to your sales presentation, attend your seminar or even call you.

If you are old enough you may remember the Fuller Brush Man, who went door to door selling brushes and I forget what else, but I do remember that my Mom got a free brush every time he came to the door. Now she had to open the door to get her free brush, boy what a door opener huh! Then the rule of reciprocity took over and my Mom usually bought something if she could.

Reason #3 your book provides an easy way to *contact prospects*, you can pop by a potential customers place of business and say that you came by to give them your book. Now the secretary or gatekeeper may not let you see the contact person you wanted to, but you can just to say; I'd like them to have my book it has solutions in it that may help your business. Do you think she is going to give your book to them? Of course she will; as there is a perception of value in a book, she's not going to throw it the trash can with the junk mail and unsolicited brochures. Saying; I'll call later to see how they liked the book, can help insure delivery to the right person and even get your call put through to the desired contact person later.

You can send your book by FedEx or priority mail, and pump up the perceived value. The secretary or gatekeeper is not going to throw the book away, matter fact she may immediately take it in to your prospect.

Reason #4 your book will *generate leads* just by having your book available to people who visit your business location, or handing out your book out at conventions, tradeshows, or the county fair. Anyplace you can hand this book out for free or offer for sale at a discount.

You will create leads by requiring contact information in exchange for the book, remember reciprocity?

Your book will act as a sales funnel, sifting and sorting the people you meet. If people have no in interest in your book title or topic they move on, if they are curious or have more interest they read on.

Reason #5 *lead conversions*, you will convert your leads into hot prospects simply by them reading the information in your book. You will provide not only possible solutions to their problems, but also suggestions and resources for them to use, including your products and services that serve as your backend. Your book will probably not make you any money it will however create hot prospects for your backend that is where you make your money.

Reason #6 Your book will *create sales* by converting hot prospects into clients or customers simply because you have shown them in your book why they need what you offer them and a way to get it..

Reason#7 is *publicity* a book gives you publicity on so many levels it can get you booked for interviews, seminars, speeches, guest on radio or TV, people will want to know more about you and what you offer.

For additional information and help with getting all of the components of your book together, please contact me:

Dale Anderson

830-243-2598

www.TheBigBusinessCard.com

www.ingramcontent.com/pod-product-compliance
Lightning Source LLC
Chambersburg PA
CBHW071120210326
41519CB00020B/6356